Persephone

This is Persephone, known as Kore, the maiden, before her abduction to the underworld by Hades, king of the land of the dead. There she became his queen. The ancient Greeks believed that after they died, they would continue to exist as shadowy spirits in the dark and gloomy realm of Hades and Persephone. Here Persephone carries branches of the pomegranate, a symbol of the afterlife and the land of the dead. Later in this book you will find out why the pomegranate was associated with Persephone.

Δημήτηρ᾽ ἠΰκομον,
σεμνὴν θεάν, ἄρχομ᾽
ἀείδειν, αὐτὴν καὶ κούρην,
περικαλλέα
Περσεφόνειαν.

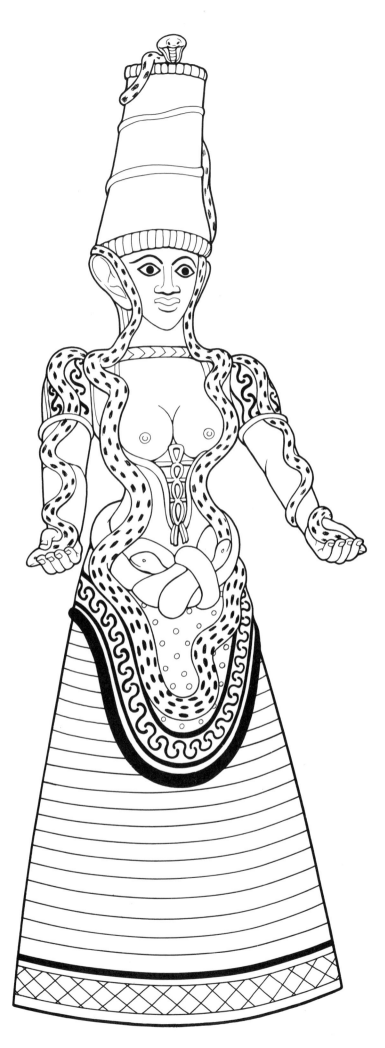

Snake
Priestesses

The oldest Greek stories are about the goddesses of nature. There were goddesses of animals, darkness, light, and the Earth. These stories helped the ancient Greeks to understand the world around them. The Greeks believed that Gaia, the Earth goddess, was the oldest and most wonderful goddess of all. She was the creator of all life on Earth, from the plants and the animals to the birds and the fish.

From a faience statuette, c. 1600 B.C. Herakleion Museum

γαῖαν παμμήτειραν
ἀείσομαι, ἠυθέμεθλον,
πρεσβίστην, ἢ φέρβει ἐπὶ
χθονὶ πάνθ' ὁπόσ' ἐστίν,

from a faience statuette, c. 1600 B.C., from the Palace of Knossos; Herakleion Musem

Here are two priestesses from the Greek island of Crete. They are carrying snakes, which symbolize the powers of the Earth goddess. The powerful priestesses are wearing special headdresses and costumes made from many layers of brightly colored fabric.

ἠμὲν ὅσα χθόνα δῖαν ἐπέρχεται ἠδ' ὅσα πόντοον ἠδ' ὅσα πωτῶνται, τάδε φέρβεται ἐκ σέθεν ὄλβου.

Ἦμος δ' ἠριγένεια φάνη
ῥοδοδάκτυλος Ἠώς,

Ἠὼς δ' ἐκ λεχέων παρ' ἀγαυοῦ
Τιθωνοῖο ὤρνυθ', ἵν' ἀθανάτοισι
φόως φέροι ἠδὲ βροτοῖσιν· οἱ δὲ
θεοὶ θῶκόνδε καθίζανον, ἐν δ'
ἄρα τοῖσι Ζεὺς ὑψιβρεμέτης, οὗ
τε κράτος ἐστὶ μέγιστον.

Eos

Eos, the granddaughter of Gaia, was the goddess of the dawn. She had rosy cheeks and fingers and wore a bright yellow gown. She flew across the sky each morning in her chariot drawn by two horses, bringing light to each new day. Eos is shown in this picture chasing the handsome prince Tithonus of Troy.

Eos wanted to marry Tithonus and live with him forever. But there was a problem! Eos, as a goddess, would live forever, but Tithonus was only a mortal man and, like all men, would die someday. Eos loved Tithonus so much that she asked her cousin Zeus, the king of the gods, to grant eternal life to Tithonus. Zeus did so, but she had forgotten to ask for eternal youth. Tithonus grew very, very old, but he was able to live with Eos forever.

Hera
(next page)

Hera was another granddaughter of Gaia, the Earth goddess. Hera married Zeus, king of the gods, and became the queen of all the goddesses. Hera was very powerful. She was the goddess of marriage and families, and she helped women to give birth to strong, healthy babies. Hera and Zeus symbolized the mother and father in the ancient Greek family, and they had several divine children.

This portrait of Hera decorated her famous temple at Olympia, home of the original Olympic games. The ancient Greek poets often called Hera "ox-eyed" because she had such big, shiny, beautiful eyes, just as she has in this picture.

From a lekythos by the Gigantomachy Painter, c. 480 B.C. Frankfurt, *Museum für Kunsthandwerk*

Τὴν δ' ἠμείβετ'
ἔπειτα βοῶπις
πότνια Ἥρα·

Hera from a limestone head, early 6th century B.C. Olympia Museum

Hera and Prometheus

From a cup by Duris, c. 475 B.C. Paris, *Cabinet des Médailles* 542

Ἥρην ἀείδω χρυσόθρονον, ἣν τέκε Ῥείη ἀθανάτων βασίλειαν,

   Here ox-eyed Hera is shown seated on her royal throne. In one hand, she is holding a golden scepter. The scepter is a symbol of her status as queen of the goddesses. She is giving a jeweled bowl to her friend Prometheus. Prometheus was a Titan who was the champion of mankind and an enemy of Hera's husband Zeus. Hera and Zeus enjoyed playing tricks and trying to fool each other. Perhaps Hera and Prometheus are discussing a trick that they will play on Zeus.

Hades, god of the underworld, is carrying the young Persephone away to be his bride. Persephone was the young daughter of the goddess Demeter, who had power over the fertility of the soil. Persephone loved to roam the Earth, admiring the flowers and singing with the birds, and she was very beautiful. Hades saw her, fell in love with her beauty, and

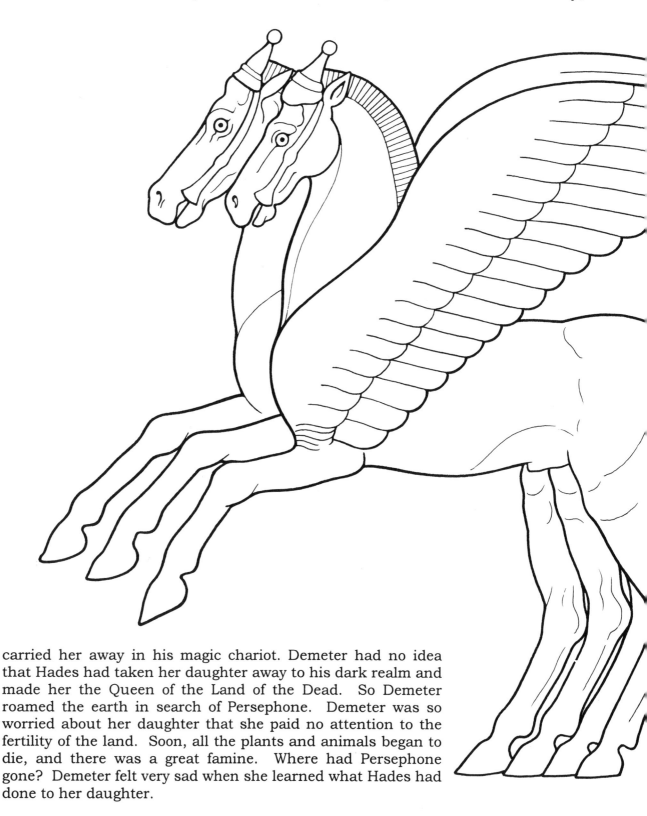

carried her away in his magic chariot. Demeter had no idea that Hades had taken her daughter away to his dark realm and made her the Queen of the Land of the Dead. So Demeter roamed the earth in search of Persephone. Demeter was so worried about her daughter that she paid no attention to the fertility of the land. Soon, all the plants and animals began to die, and there was a great famine. Where had Persephone gone? Demeter felt very sad when she learned what Hades had done to her daughter.

Persephone and Hades

From a terracotta relief from Locri, c. 460 B.C. Taranto, *Museo Nazionale*

Next page:

Hades and Persephone are holding plants and other objects that identify them as king and queen of the dead. Persephone was unhappy living with Hades in his dark realm, but she could not return to the world above because she had eaten a pomegranate seed in the underworld. Once her mother Demeter found out what had happened to Persephone, she complained to Zeus. In order to make everyone happy, Zeus decreed that Persephone should be allowed to remain with her mother for part of the year, but must return to live with Hades the rest of the time. The ancient Greeks believed that this was the reason for winter—a time when Demeter is sad because her daughter is in the underworld.

αὐτὴν ἡδὲ θύγατρα τανύσφυρον, ἣν ᾿αιδωνεὺς ἥρπαξεν, δῶκεν δὲ βαρύκτυπος
εὐρύοπα Ζεύς, νόσφιν Δήμητρος χρυσαόρου, ἀγλαοκάρπου,

Ἀργειφόντην, ὄφρ' Ἀΐδην μαλακοῖσι
παραιφάμενος ἐπέεσσιν ἁγνὴν Περσεφόνειαν.

Persephone
and Hades

From a terracotta relief from Locri, c. 470 B.C.
Reggio Calabria, *Museo Nazionale*

Demeter with Baby Demophoön

From a terracotta relief from Locri, c. 470 B.C. Reggio Calabria, *Museo Nazionale*

Δημήτηρ χρίεσκ᾽ ἀμβροσίῃ ὡς εἰ θεοῦ ἐκγεγαῶτα,
ἡδὺ καταπνείουσα καὶ ἐν κόλποισιν ἔχουσα·

While Demeter was wandering the earth in search of her daughter Persephone, she disguised herself as a mortal woman. The king and queen of the city of Eleusis took her in—not knowing she was really a goddess—and employed her as a nurse for their little baby son Demophoön. Demeter loved the young prince and took good care of him.

Because of the kindness of the king and queen and the fondness that Demeter had for Demophoön, Eleusis became the most important place for the worship of Demeter.

Demeter

Triptolemu

From a cup by Makron, c. 490 B.C.
London, British Museum E 140

Persephone

Triptolemus was a hero from the city of Eleusis, which held a special place in the heart of Demeter. She was said to have taught the art of agriculture to Triptolemus, who then flew on his chariot around the world to spread his new knowledge among the peoples of the earth.

ἠμὲν Τριπτολέμου πυκιμήδεος ἠδὲ Διόκλου
ἠδὲ Πολυξείνου καὶ ἀμύμονος Εὐμόλποιο καὶ
Δολίχου καὶ πατρὸς ἀγήνορος ἡμετέροιο
τῶν πάντων ἄλοχοι κατὰ δώματα
πορσαίνουσι·

Birth of
Aphrodite

ὣς φέρετ' ἄμ πέλαγος πουλὺν
χρόνον, ἀμφὶ δὲ λευκὸς ἀφρὸς
ἀπ' ἀθανάτου χροὸς ὤρνυτο·
τῷ δ' ἔνι κούρη ἐθρέφθη·

Goddess of
love and beauty,
Aphrodite was born
from the foam of the
sea (*aphros* in Greek)
from which she rises up,
here, helped by servants who
cover her with beautiful clothes.

From the Ludovisi Throne, c. 465, Rome, *Museo Nazionale delle Terme*

Aphrodite
with Cupid and Pan

From a mirror, c. 370 B.C. London, British Museum 289

μοῦσά μοι ἔννεπε ἔργα πολυχρύσου Ἀφροδίτης,
Κύπριδος, ἥτε θεοῖσιν ἐπὶ γλυκὺν ἵμερον ὦρσε

    Aphrodite is playing a game with Pan, a wild, woodland deity who always tried to make Aphrodite fall in love with him—it never worked! On Aphrodite's left is Eros, a young, winged god who often helped Aphrodite make people fall in love by shooting his arrows. Maybe here he is trying to help old Pan out.

Aphrodite on a Swan

The ancient Greeks associated the swan with Aphrodite because
swans are both graceful and powerful, just like Aphrodite herself.

καί τ' ἐδαμάσσατο φῦλα καταθνητῶν ἀνθρώπων οἰωνούς τε διιπετέας καὶ θηρία πάντα,

ἔνθά σφιν λιπαροί τε χοροὶ καὶ
δώματα καλά, πὰρ δ᾽ αὐτῆς
Χάριτές τε καὶ Ἵμερος οἰκί᾽
ἔχουσιν ἐν θαλίῃς·

From a marble relief by Kallimachos
c. 400 B.C., Rome, Capitoline Museum

The Three Graces

The three Graces, or Charites, are personifications of grace and style. Daughters of Zeus and a sea nymph named Eurynome, they often accompanied the goddess Aphrodite, or danced with the Muses in the Olympian meadows. Aglaia personified radiance; Euphrosne, joy; and Thalia, the blooming of flowers.

"But, above all things, to all that you learn, to all that you say, and to all that you do, remember to join the *Graces.* All that is imperfect without them. . .

Invoke them, and sacrifice to them every moment; they are always kind, where they are assiduously courted."

—*Lord Chesterfield*, 1750

For much more,
see Bellerophon's magnificent
Book of Good Manners.

Birth of Athena

Athena was born from the head of Zeus! An oracle told Zeus that a woman he loved named Metis would have a child greater than its father. Zeus became frightened and swallowed Metis. Some time later, Zeus had a terrible headache and finally Athena popped out of his forehead, wearing her helmet and armor, and carrying a spear—ouch!

From a pelike by the Athena-birth Painter, c. 465 B.C. London, British Museum E 410

παρθένον αἰδοίην, ἐρυσίπτολιν,
ἀλκήεσσαν, Τριτογενῆ, τὴν
αὐτὸς ἐγείνατο μητίετα Ζεὺς
σεμνῆς ἐκ κεφαλῆς, πολεμήια
τεύχε᾽ ἔχουσαν,

Athena

From a fragment of a cup by the Eleusis
Painter, c. 500 B.C. Eleusis 619

Athena is brandishing a spear as
she fights in battle. Unlike the
other goddesses, Athena is a
fighter. She had powers over
strategy in war, and she often
advised and protected the Greek
heroes in their adventures and
battles. The cape she wears here
is called the "aegis"—it was given
to her by her father, Zeus. It was
fringed with snakes and had a
terrible Gorgon's head in the
middle. It made her invincible!

Παλλάδ' 'Αθηναίην
ἐρυσίπτολιν ἄρχομ'
ἀείδειν, δεινήν, ἧ σὺν
"Αρηι μέλει πολεμήια
ἔργα

Gaia
Erichthonius & Athena

The goddess Athena, on the right, receives a baby called Erichthonius from his mother Gaia, the Earth Goddess. Erichthonius was raised by Athena and eventually became King of Athens. Because of the close relationship of Athena and Erichthonius the city of Athens became devoted to the worship of the goddess.

ἐπὶ χθονὶ πάνθ'
ὁπόσ' ἐστίν,

From a kylix by the Kodros Painter, c. 435 B.C., Berlin-Charlottenburg F 2537

Myth to History:

Oreithyia & Boreas

Βορέας τὴν Ὠρείθυιαν ἀρπάσαι;

Oreithyia, daughter of King Erechtheus of Athens, was playing along the banks of the Ilissus River. Boreas, the God of the North Wind, swept down in a blast of cold air and carried her away to make her his wife! Their sons, Calais and Zetes, accompanied Jason and the argonauts on their voyage in search of the Golden Fleece.

From an amphora by the Oreithyia Painter, c. 475 B.C., Munich 2345

From the Altar of Zeus from Pergamon, c.180 B.C. Berlin, Pergamon Museum

χρύσεα, παμφανόωντα·
σέβας δ' ἔχε πάντας
ὁρῶντας ἀθανάτους· ἢ δὲ
πρόσθεν Διὸς αἰγιόχοιο
ἐσσυμένως ὤρουσεν ἀπ'
ἀθανάτοιο καρήνου,

Athena and Gaia

The giant race of titans, led by Alcyoneus, once attempted to overthrow the gods and goddesses of Olympus, but the gods fought back mightily. Here Alcyoneus is shown struggling with Athena as his mother the earth goddess Gaia looks on helplessly. However, Alcyoneus was invincible against all weapons made by the gods. In the end, Athena called on the hero Heracles to enter the fray, and he slew Alcyoneus with his arrows.

The titaness Leto was the kindest and gentlest of all the gods. Yet even she was not spared from the wrath of the jealous Hera who discovered that Zeus was the father of Leto's unborn twins. She pursued Leto to the ends of the earth, forbidding her to touch land to give birth. Leto finally found refuge on the Aegean island of Delos and gave birth to her children, Apollo and Artemis.

Leto

Apollo

From an amphora c. 700 B.C. Athens, National Museum 5898

Apollo and Artemis were among the most important of the Greek gods, with great shrines at Delphi and Delos. Apollo represented archery, medicine, the arts, and the virtues of civilization—order and harmony. Artemis watched over childbirth and animals.

Artemis

αἵ μὲν 'Απόλλων' ὑμνήσωσιν, αὖτις δ' αὖ Λητώ τε καὶ Ἄρτεμιν ἰοχέαιραν,

Artemis

Artemis was called the Mistress of the Animals, especially the deer and bear. Here, she appears in her role as goddess of the hunt, wearing a deerskin. She is carrying a magnificent quiver, from which she has pulled two golden arrows as she prepares to draw her mighty bow. In an equally contradictory fashion, Artemis, a free and independent spirit who never married, relieved the suffering of women in childbirth and was a protector and nurturer of children.

Ἄρτεμιν ἀείδω χρυσηλάκατον,
κελαδεινήν, παρθένον αἰδοίην,
ἐλαφηβόλον, ἰοχέαιραν,

From a krater by the Pan Painter, c. 470 B.C.
Boston, Museum of Fine Arts 10.185

καὶ γάρ τ' ἠΰκομος Νιόβη ἐμνήσατο
σίτου, τῇ περ δώδεκα παῖδες ἐνὶ
μεγάροισιν ὅλοντο ἒξ μὲν θυγατέρες,
ἒξ δ' υἱέες ἡβώοντες.

Artemis

Artemis attacks giants. As always, Artemis carries her hunting bow and a quiver of arrows—she has shot her last one. Her faithful dog is biting a terrible serpent with the head of a man. At the goddess's feet lies another earthborn giant, smitten. Giants and monsters opposed Artemis and her Olympian siblings in their attempts to rise to power. As you can see, they failed.

From the Pergamon altar, c. 180 B.C., Pergamon Museum, Berlin

Niobe

From a marble copy after Skopas, c. 320 B.C.
Florence, *Museo degli Uffizi*

τοὺς μὲν Ἀπόλλων
πέφνεν ἀπ' ἀργυρέοιο
βιοῖο χωόμενος Νιόβῃ,
τὰς δ' Ἄρτεμις ἰοχέαιρα.

Niobe, a mortal woman, was the mother of at least six sons and six daughters. She was proud—too proud—and dared to compare herself to the goddess Leto, at whom she scoffed for having only two children. Angry, Leto sent Apollo and Artemis to punish her. With her arrows, Artemis killed all Niobe's daughters— Niobe tries in vain to save one here—and Apollo slew the sons as they were hunting. So saddened was Niobe that she wept until she turned into a pillar of stone. Even today you can see the weeping rock on Mount Sipylus in Turkey.

ἥ δ' ὑποκυσαμένη
Ἑκάτην τέκε.

Hecate

Triple-bodied Hecate, goddess of the crossroads, was most highly honored by Zeus. She was associated with magic and the underworld. Here she battles the giant Clytios.

From the Pergamon altar, c. 180 B.C., Pergamon Museum, Berlin

A **lion-goddess** joins Artemis in her battle against the monstrous race of giants.

Pergamon altar

Atalanta

Atalanta stands in an athletic arena, dressed for competition. She had been nursed by a bear and raised by hunters. When she grew up, she became a follower of Artemis. She could run faster than anyone else alive.

τελεία δὲ Ἀταλάντη γενομένη παρθένον ἑαυτὴν

Atalanta, dressed in a beautiful, finely woven gown, is running her race to escape love. She looks back to see how close her opponent is. Will he catch her?

Nike of Paeonius

Nike, goddess of victory, flies down from the gods' home on Mount Olympus. She fought on the side of the gods in their struggle against the giants and personified their victory over them. Here, she carries a wreath of olive leaves to crown the winners of the Olympic Games.

Atalanta liked being an athlete, and she swore that she would never marry. But her father insisted that she must, so Atalanta finally agreed to marry any man who could defeat her in a foot race—but any man that lost to her had to be put to death! Several youths lost and were killed, but one young man, Hippomenes, tricked her by dropping golden apples on the track—something that Atalanta could not resist. She slowed down to pick up the pretty golden apples, and he was able to run past her and win her as his bride.

Στύξ δ' ἔτεκ'
Ὡκεανοᾶ θυγάτηρ
Πάλλαντι μιγεῖσα
Ζῆλον κα" Νίκην
καλλίσφυρον ἱν
μεγάροισιν

From the statue of Nike by Paeonius of Mende, 421 B.C., which stood by the temple of Zeus at Olympia on a base that was more than thirty feet high. When the visitors came to see the Olympic Games, they could look into the sky above them and see the goddess of victory coming down to join them.

Eris

From a little-master cup, c. 560 B.C. Berlin-Charlottenburg F 1775

Eris, the goddess of strife and discord, is shown rushing off to create mischief and havoc. She was a daughter of the goddess of night, and she was the mother of Toil, Forgetfulness, Hunger, Pain, Battle, Bloodshed, Lies, Ruin, and Delusion. Her most famous moment was at the wedding of Peleus and Thetis. Eris came to the wedding banquet—even though she wasn't invited—and brought with her a golden apple, on which was written "for the fairest." A contest followed between the goddesses Athena, Hera, and Aphrodite to decide which of them should be given the apple. The judge was the Trojan prince Paris, who was successfully bribed by Aphrodite. Athena and Hera were angry with Paris and plotted against Troy. The result was the Trojan War. αὐτὰρ Ἔρις στυγερὴ τέκε μὲν Πόνον ἀλγινόεντα

Sphinx and Oedipus

From a cup by the Oedipus Painter, c. 470 B.C. Vatican Museum 569

Οἰδίπους δὲ ἀκούσας
ἔλυσεν, εἰπὼν τὸ
αἴνιγμα τὸ ὑπὸ τῆς
Σφιγγός.

The Sphinx was a terrible monster with the head of a woman, the body of a lion, and the wings of a bird. Descending on the city of Thebes, she wreaked great destruction and said that she would not leave until someone answered this riddle: "What goes on four legs in the morning, two at midday, and three in the evening?" Many men took a guess, but all answered incorrectly and were devoured by the Sphinx. Finally, the hero Oedipus gave the correct answer: "Man." The Sphinx threw herself to death, and Oedipus became king of the city he had saved.

Europa

The beautiful princess Europa lived in the city of Tyre, on the coast of Phoenicia. One day as she and her companions played on the seashore, Zeus saw her and fell instantly in love. He transformed himself into a handsome snow-white bull and approached her. Tame and gentle, he won her trust, and Europa climbed on his back. Then, still in the form of a bull, Zeus plunged into the waves and carried her across the sea to the island of Crete.

Europa's brother Cadmus greatly missed his sister and searched for her, but without much success. Finally, he consulted the Oracle of Apollo at Delphi, who assured him Europa was safe. He was also told to follow a certain cow and to build a city where it rested; this city became Thebes. Cadmus named the surrounding area after his sister. Later, the entire continent of Europe would bear her name.

Κάδμος γὰρ ὁ ᾽Αγήνορος Εὐρώπην
διζήμενος προσέσχε ἐς τὴν νῦν Θήρην
καλεομένην· προσσχόντι δὲ εἴτε δή οἱ ἡ
χώρη ἤρεσε

From a Caeretan hydria, c. 520 B.C. Rome, *Villa Giulia Museo*

From a hydria by the Coghill Painter, c. 450 B.C. London, British Museum 2170

Apollo

Ἀπόλλωνα δὲ Δάφνη ἐπ' αὐτὴν ἰόντα προϊδομένη μάλα
ἐρρωμένως ἔφευγεν. ὡς δὲ συνεδιώκετο, παρὰ Διὸς αἰτεῖται ἐξ
ἀνθρώπων ἀπαλλαγῆναι. καὶ αὐτήν φασι γενέσθαι τὸ δένδρον
τὸ ἐπικληθὲν ἀπ' ἐκείνης δάφνην.

    Here a nymph called Daphne is being chased by the god Apollo, who carries a
staff from a laurel tree in his right hand. Apollo had fallen in love with Daphne,
but she didn't love him in return. Daphne was the daughter of a river god in
Arcadia, and she prayed to her father for help in escaping Apollo. Her father

and Daphne

obliged by turning her into a laurel tree (Daphne means "laurel tree" in Greek) just at the point when Apollo was about to catch her. Ever after Apollo wore a garland of leaves from a laurel in commemoration of his love for the beautiful nymph who had escaped him.

"Ήβην δ' Ἀλκμήνος καλλισφύρου ἄλκιμος υἱός, ἲς Ἡρακλῆος, τελέσας στονόεντας ἀέθλους,

Hebe and Himeros

Hebe, or Youth, is handed an amphora of perfume by Himeros, or Desire. It may have been that which inspired Heracles to marry her.

From a knee cover for carding wool by the Eretria Painter, c. 420 B.C., Athens, National Museum

καὶ Ζεὺς μὲν αἰσθόμενος
κτείνει Κούρητας, Ἰὼ δὲ
ἐπὶ ζήτησιν τοῦ παιδὸς
ἐτράπετο.

Io

Io was one of Hera's favorite priestesses. Zeus fell in love with the beautiful Io and Hera became very jealous and angry. She turned Io into a white cow and ordered the hundred-eyed Argus to watch her carefully. Io managed to escape, but she wandered the earth for many years, tormented by a gadfly sent by jealous Hera. When Io reached Egypt after many years of wandering, Zeus returned her to human form. Io was the grandmother of the Egyptian goddess Isis, who also wore horns

From a pelike by the Io Painter, c. 455 B.C. Spinelli 2041

From a bobbin by the Pistoxenos Painter, c. 470 B.C. Athens, National Museum 2192

Thetis and Peleus

The lovely goddess Thetis is being courted by the famous hero Peleus as a friendly dolphin swims nearby. Thetis was a sea nymph, a daughter of the sea god Nereus. The wedding of Peleus and Thetis was the event of the ages, and it was attended by both the gods and the leading mortals of the day. It was there that Eris, goddess of strife and discord, initiated the contest which would lead to the Trojan war.

Here Thetis works her magic—she was a goddess after all—and makes snakes and a lion appear around Peleus. Their son, Achilles, was the greatest and most famous of all the Greek heroes. While Achilles was fighting at Troy, his mother Thetis regularly acted as a mediator between her son and the gods. Zeus was very fond of Thetis and usually agreed to whatever she asked. It is even said that she and Zeus plotted to start the war just to provide a situation in which her son could prove himself the greatest hero of all time. That's a devoted mom!

Τὸν δ' ἠμείβετ' ἔπειτα Θέτις κατὰ δάκρυ χέουσα· ὤ μοι τέκνον ἐμόν, τί
νύ σ' ἔτρεφον αἰνὰ τεκοῦσα; αἴθ' ὄφελες παρὰ νηυσὶν ἀδάκρυτος·

Pasiphaë and the Minotaur

Pasiphaë, the wife of King Minos of Crete, sits with her son, the Minotaur, in her lap. Pasiphaë had been enchanted by Zeus, who appeared to her in the disguise of a bull. As a result, she gave birth to the Minotaur, a monster that was part human and part bull. Pasiphaë was also the mother of Ariadne, who ran off with the Athenian hero Theseus after he killed the Minotaur.

Πασιφάη γάρ, ἐπειδὴ πολλαῖς Μίνως συνηυνάζετο γυναιξίν, ἐφαρμάκευσεν αὐτόν.

Theseus and Ariadne

Ariadne hands the Athenian hero Theseus a ball of twine that he will use to find his way out of the treacherous maze of the Labyrinth. King Minos of Crete had sent Theseus into the dreadful Labyrinth, where a terrible monster called the Minotaur lived. No one had ever survived an encounter with the Minotaur, but Theseus had help from Ariadne! She was the daughter of King Minos of Crete and had fallen in love with Theseus, so she helped him defeat the Minotaur—and then she ran off with him on his way back to Athens. Theseus betrayed her and left her alone on the island of Naxos, where the god Dionysus rescued and married her. Δαίδαλος ἤσκησεν καλλιπλοκάμῳ Ἀριάδνῃ. ἔνθα μὲν ἠΐθεοι καὶ παρθένοι ἀλφεσίβοιο

Night

From a cup by the Brygos Painter, c. 485 B.C. Berlin-Charlottenburg

ἐκ Χάεος δ' Ἔρεβός τε μέλαινά τε Νὺξ ἐγένοντο·

    The goddess Nyx rides her chariot of winged horses through the starry heavens. Nyx (the night) and Erebos (the darkness) were born from Chaos (the void), at the beginning of time, before Zeus and the other Olympian gods were born. It was from Nyx and Erebos that Aethere (the brightness in the sky) and Henera (the day) were born. Nyx also produced Nemesis, the goddess of retribution for injustice and the Moerae, or Fates, who decide when people are born, how long they live, and the time of their death.